M000190844

Pain Pushed Me Into My Purpose

WALKED THROUGH THE FIRE
BUT NOT BURNED

A poetry memoir by

SHAKIRA MCGEE

ISBN: 978-1-09836-057-3

Introduction

ISAIAH 54

54 Sing, O barren, thou that didst not bear; break forth into singing, and cry aloud, thou that didst not travail with child: for more are the children of the desolate than the children of the married wife, saith the Lord.

² Enlarge the place of thy tent, and let them stretch forth the curtains of thine habitations: spare not, lengthen thy cords, and strengthen thy stakes;

³ For thou shalt break forth on the right hand and on the left; and thy seed shall inherit the Gentiles, and make the desolate cities to be inhabited.

⁴ Fear not; for thou shalt not be ashamed: neither be thou confounded; for thou shalt not be put to shame: for thou shalt forget the shame of thy youth, and shalt not remember the reproach of thy widowhood any more.

⁵ For thy Maker is thine husband; the Lord of hosts is his name; and thy Redeemer the Holy One of Israel; The God of the whole earth shall he be called.

6 For the Lord hath called thee as a woman forsaken and grieved in spirit, and a wife of youth, when thou wast refused, saith thy God.

7 For a small moment have I forsaken thee; but with great mercies will I gather thee.

8 In a little wrath I hid my face from thee for a moment; but with everlasting kindness will I have mercy on thee, saith the Lord thy Redeemer.

9 For this is as the waters of Noah unto me: for as I have sworn that the waters of Noah should no more go over the earth; so have I sworn that I would not be wroth with thee, nor rebuke thee.

10 For the mountains shall depart, and the hills be removed; but my kindness shall not depart from thee, neither shall the covenant of my peace be removed, saith the Lord that hath mercy on thee.

11 O thou afflicted, tossed with tempest, and not comforted, behold, I will lay thy stones with fair colours, and lay thy foundations with sapphires.

¹² And I will make thy windows of agates, and thy gates of carbuncles, and all thy borders of pleasant stones.

¹³ And all thy children shall be taught of the Lord; and great shall be the peace of thy children.

¹⁴ In righteousness shalt thou be established: thou shalt be far from oppression; for thou shalt not fear: and from terror; for it shall not come near thee.

¹⁵ Behold, they shall surely gather together, but not by me: whosoever shall gather together against thee shall fall for thy sake.

¹⁶ Behold, I have created the smith that bloweth the coals in the fire, and that bringeth forth an instrument for his work; and I have created the waster to destroy.

¹⁷ No weapon that is formed against thee shall prosper; and every tongue that shall rise against thee in judgment thou shalt condemn. This is the heritage of the servants of the Lord, and their righteousness is of me, saith the Lord.

Table of Contents

Pain Pushed Me Into My Purpose

WALKED THROUGH THE FIRE

BUT NOT BURNED

Self-Love

All the while,
you weren't the one loving me.

I was busy learning
to love myself.

Facing my deepest pain
of being alone
is where I found codependency
and knew I did not
want her to be my home.

My heart started to grieve,
which opened up
a hidden door to my brokenness.
A door I'd sealed shut
and never wanted to be open.

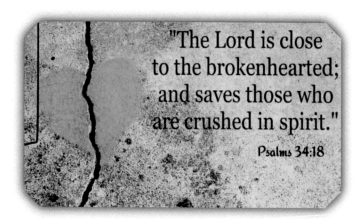

"The Lord is close to the brokenhearted; and saves those who are crushed in spirit."

Psalms 34:18

Healing Process

Mourning the loss
of what I held on to
for so many years
had my pillow
not only soaked
but drenched in tears.

I realized this was a pain
I had to feel.
So that I could get the closure
I desperately needed
and let my heart finally heal.

The pain took me through
different stages of my past.
I thought to myself,
Lord how long will this last?

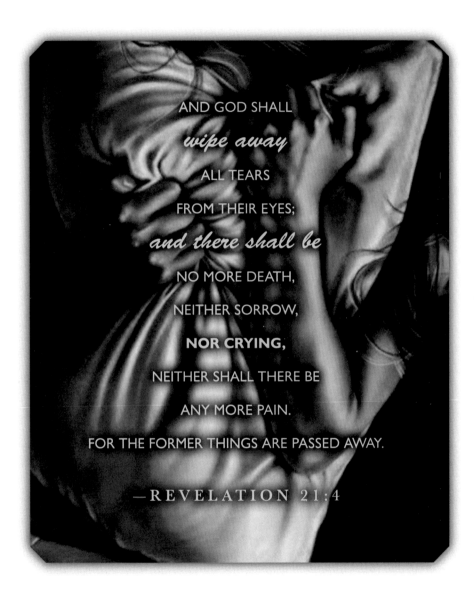

AND GOD SHALL

wipe away

ALL TEARS

FROM THEIR EYES;

and there shall be

NO MORE DEATH,

NEITHER SORROW,

NOR CRYING,

NEITHER SHALL THERE BE

ANY MORE PAIN.

FOR THE FORMER THINGS ARE PASSED AWAY.

—REVELATION 21:4

Learning Who I Am in Christ

I needed
true happiness
that comes
only from within.

So, as she crept in,
I had no problem embracing her,
like my new best friend.

I stumbled across insecurity
when I felt the need to be validated,
which honestly made things worse
and much more complicated.

I KNEW YOU BEFORE I formed YOU IN YOUR MOTHER'S WOMB. BEFORE YOU WERE BORN I SET YOU apart.

JEREMIAH 1:5

Recognizing My Worth

But, that's how I met my worth.

Knowing I deserved more than what I was getting.

Having to face reality that really hurt.

Stuck; Can't Move Forward

I was struck by
bitterness,
unforgiveness,
and resentment
along the way,
which I knew was only hurting me.
So, they definitely couldn't stay.

LETTING GO AND GOING ON

Ephesians 4:31 Let all bitterness, and wrath, and anger, and clamour, and evil speaking, be put away from you, with all malice: 32 And be ye kind one to another, tenderhearted, forgiving one another, even as God for Christ's sake hath forgiven you.

Healed

After this process,
Is where I found Mr. Heal.
By this time,
I was weak and vulnerable.
So now, I feel.
I fell in love with Mr. Heal
and here came Mrs. Whole.

I will give you
a new heart
and put a new spirit
in you;
I will remove
from you
your heart of stone
and give you
a heart of flesh.
NIV®

Ezekiel 36:26

Becoming Whole

Showing me,
I could never be complete
without God filling the void.

I pray that out of his glorious riches he may strengthen you with power through his Spirit in your inner being, so that Christ may dwell in your hearts through faith.

I pray that you, being rooted and established in love... may be filled to the measure of all the fullness of God.

Ephesians 3:16-19

Breakthrough

Searching for freedom,
I started breaking bonds and chains.
It was during those trials
and sufferings
that God gave me my new name.

Knowing Who I Am in Christ

I had found my identity in Christ
and no longer
wanted to stay the same.

I AM ACCEPTED

JOHN 1:12	I AM GOD'S CHILD.
JOHN 15:15	AS A DISCIPLE, I AM A FRIEND OF JESUS CHRIST.
ROM 5:1	I HAVE BEEN JUSTIFIED.
1 COR 6:17	I AM UNITED WITH THE LORD, AND ONE WITH HIM IN SPIRIT.
1 COR 6:19-20	I HAVE BEEN BOUGHT WITH A PRICE AND I BELONG TO GOD.
1 COR 12:27	I AM A MEMBER OF CHRIST'S BODY.
EPH 1:3-8	I HAVE BEEN CHOSEN BY GOD AND ADOPTED AS HIS CHILD.
COL 1:13-14	I HAVE BEEN REDEEMED AND FORGIVEN OF ALL MY SINS.
COL 2:9-10	I AM COMPLETE IN CHRIST.
HEB 4:14-16	I HAVE DIRECT ACCESS TO THE THRONE OF GRACE THROUGH JESUS CHRIST.

I AM SECURE

ROM 8:1-2	I AM FREE FROM CONDEMNATION
ROM 9:28	I AM ASSURED THAT GOD WORKS GOOD IN ALL CIRCUMSTANCES
ROM 8:31-39	I AM FREE FROM ANY CONDEMNATION AND CANNOT BE SEPARATED FROM THE LOVE OF GOD
2 COR 1:21-22	I HAVE BEEN ESTABLISHED, ANOINTED AND SEALED BY GOD
COL 3:1-4	I AM HIDDEN WITH CHRIST IN GOD
PHIL 1:6	I AM CONFIDENT THAT GOD WILL COMPLETE THE GOOD WORK HE STARTED IN ME
2 TIM 1:7	I HAVE NOT BEEN GIVEN A SPIRIT OF FEAR BUT OF POWER, LOVE AND A SOUND MIND
1 JOHN 5:18	I AM BORN OF GOD AND THE EVIL ONE CANNOT TOUCH ME

I AM SIGNIFICANT

JOHN 15:5	I AM A BRANCH OF JESUS CHRIST THE TRUE VINE
JOHN 15:6	I HAVE BEEN CHOSEN AND APPOINTED TO BEAR FRUIT
1 COR 3:16	I AM GOD'S TEMPLE
2 COR 5:17-21	I AM A MINISTER OF RECONCILIATION FOR GOD
EPH 2:6	I AM SEATED WITH JESUS CHRIST IN THE HEAVENLY REALM
EPH 3:10	I MAY APPROACH GOD WITH FREEDOM AND CONFIDENCE
PHIL 4:13	I CAN DO ALL THINGS THROUGH CHRIST WHO STRENGTHENS ME
1 JOHN 5:18	I AM BORN OF GOD AND THE EVIL ONE CANNOT TOUCH ME

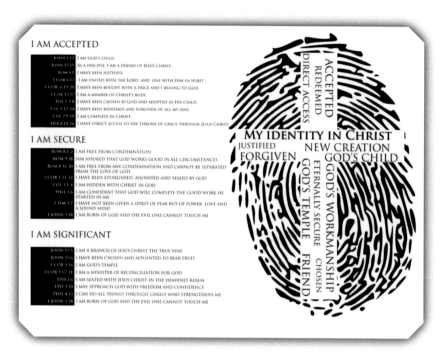

MY IDENTITY IN CHRIST

ACCEPTED
REDEEMED
DIRECT ACCESS

JUSTIFIED
FORGIVEN

NEW CREATION
GOD'S CHILD

GOD'S WORKMANSHIP
ETERNALLY SECURE
GOD'S TEMPLE
CHOSEN
FRIEND

Surrender Totally

Realizing I was standing
on holy ground
and had to take off my shoes.

Surrendering everything
was probably one of the hardest things
I had to do.
But, hey!
What could I stand to lose?
I already played the fool.

I tried it my way for so many years.
Until, I just wanted to let go
and let God wipe away my tears.

Finally Free, Whole, and Happy

See what the enemy didn't know
while he was planning for my downfall.
A righteous man may fall seven times
but get back up.
Even if he had to crawl.

Accepting that God is my source,
my provider,
and my help.

I have learned to put my trust
and faith
in him alone
and no one else.

Epilogue

⁴³ And a woman having an issue of blood twelve years, which had spent all her living upon physicians, neither could be healed of any,

⁴⁴ Came behind him, and touched the border of his garment: and immediately her issue of blood stanched.

⁴⁵ And Jesus said, Who touched me? When all denied, Peter and they that were with him said, Master, the multitude throng thee and press thee, and sayest thou, Who touched me?

46 And Jesus said, Somebody hath touched me: for I perceive that virtue is gone out of me.

47 And when the woman saw that she was not hid, she came trembling, and falling down before him, she declared unto him before all the people for what cause she had touched him, and how she was healed immediately.

48 And he said unto her, Daughter, be of good comfort: thy faith hath made thee whole; go in peace. Luke 8:43-48

Author Bio

Shakira McGee is a Daughter of the most High, (One and only God) A Servant Leader, A Survivor, A Victor, and A Warrior. Who has overcome many obstacles. Not in her own strength but by the power of the Lord and his saving grace. She has learned to stop using carnal weapons and start fighting with the sword of the spirit. (Word of God) That's how you win! Greater is he that is in you than he that is in the world. Jesus already overcame the world.